D1709307

The Discovery Books are prepared
under the educational supervision of

Mary C. Austin, Ed.D.
Professor of Education
University of Hawaii
Honolulu

A DISCOVERY BOOK

GARRARD PUBLISHING COMPANY
CHAMPAIGN, ILLINOIS

Linda Richards

First American Trained Nurse

by David R. Collins

illustrated by Cary

Library of Congress Cataloging in Publication Data

Collins, David R.
    Linda Richards: first American trained nurse.

    (A Discovery book)
    SUMMARY: A brief biography of the woman whose concern
for the sick led her to become the first professional
nurse in the United States in 1873.

    1. Richards, Linda Ann Judson, 1841-1930—Juvenile
literature. [1. Richards, Linda Ann Judson, 1841-1930.
2. Nurses and nursing—Biography]   I. Cary, Louis F.,
1915-   illus.   II. Title. [DNLM: 1. History of
nursing—Biography. WZ 100 R5166C 1973]

RT37.R6C64   610.73′092′4 [B] [92]   73–5889
ISBN 0-8116-6313-2

Contents

Chapter *1*

"Teach Me More"

Christmas Day, 1850.

A light snow blew across the fields of Vermont. Set between low hills, a frozen lake sparkled in the sun. The cold air rang with the shouts and laughter of boys and girls skating in circles on the ice.

In a small gray farmhouse nearby, nine-year-old Linda Richards watched the fun from a bedroom window. She smiled and waved at three of her friends walking by toward the lake.

"Linda," called a weak voice from

across the room. "Linda, I dropped my pills."

Linda turned and hurried toward the bed in the corner.

"Oh, mama, you shouldn't try to get them," she said. "I'll take care of you."

As a young girl Linda Richards many times said the words "I'll take care of you." But she did not know that with those words she was setting the pattern for her life.

Melinda Ann Judson Richards was born July 27, 1841, on a farm near Potsdam, New York. When Linda was four years old, her father moved the family west to Wisconsin. He built a log cabin and cleared land for a farm.

Linda liked her new home. With her two older sisters, Laura and Elizabeth,

Linda shared many adventures. Some days the three girls picked berries and climbed trees. Other times they went wading in streams. Each of the girls had her own hiding places in the nearby woods.

But the happy days in Wisconsin did not last. One night Mr. Richards suddenly became ill. By morning he was dead. Sadly Mrs. Richards brought her three girls back East. She bought a small farm outside Newport, Vermont, near the farm of Linda's Grandpa Sinclair.

Within a few weeks Mrs. Richards also became ill. Grandpa Sinclair drove his buggy over and helped with the outside work. The three girls shared the chores inside the farmhouse before and after school.

Laura, who was fourteen, divided the

duties among her sisters and herself. The list was long. There was little playtime for thirteen-year-old Elizabeth and nine-year-old Linda. The three girls had to make and mend clothes, cook meals, scrub floors, wash dishes, pump water, and churn butter. They all tried to care for Mrs. Richards, but Linda seemed to be the best nurse.

"Eat just a bite more," Linda would coax her mother at mealtime. "And drink a bit of Laura's good hot broth."

Without being told, Linda knew the best way to fix the pillows. She seemed to know when her mother wanted a shawl around her shoulders.

Old Doc Currier, who had an office in Newport, stopped by weekly at the Richards house. On one visit he watched Linda as she arranged the medicines on a bedside table.

"You do more good for your mother than my medicine," Doc Currier said. "But don't forget to look after yourself, child. Try to keep up with your school lessons. That will help keep your mother happy too."

Linda followed Doc Currier's orders. Every night after supper she read her lessons with Laura and Elizabeth.

Even with Linda's care, Mrs. Richards grew weaker. One spring night she called her three daughters into her room. Quietly the sick woman talked about the happy days in Wisconsin. Then, with her children beside her, Mrs. Richards died.

For many days Linda was too unhappy to talk. She did not want to eat. Sleep came after hours of crying. It was old Doc Currier who finally comforted the sad young girl.

One day he found Linda sitting alone on the front steps. He sat down beside her

"Linda, you did all you could," he said kindly. "You did more than any one of us to help your mother."

Linda shook her head.

"But it still wasn't enough," she said.

"You did everything you knew to do."

Linda looked up at the old doctor.

"I want to know more. I want to help other people who are sick. Will you teach me more?"

"I'd like to do that, Linda. Let's talk about it again when you're a little older."

Chapter 2

Barnyard Hospital

New homes were found for the Richards girls. Laura went to Boston to live with cousins. Elizabeth and Linda moved in with Grandpa and Grandma Sinclair.

Elizabeth helped Grandma Sinclair with the housework. Linda enjoyed helping grandpa with the farm animals. Soon all the animals seemed like friends to her.

As she milked the cows or fed the horses, she talked to them and called them by name. When she gathered the eggs, the hens seemed to cluck a greeting. Whatever chore she was doing, she had good company. Her pet rooster followed her everywhere on the farm.

When Linda wasn't helping with the farm chores, Grandpa Sinclair knew where to find her. One corner of the barn was special to Linda. There she cared for her animal "patients."

"If I get sick, will you take good care of me like that?" Grandpa Sinclair teased as he watched Linda spoon-feed a baby rabbit. "You nurse these rabbits and chicks and birds as if they were your own babies."

Doc Currier stopped by as often as he could. He enjoyed watching Linda work with the animals.

"You've got a good barnyard hospital here," he laughed. "I wouldn't mind being a sick cow on this farm."

"You're just like grandpa," Linda said. "I'm glad my animal patients don't tease me all the time."

Other people heard about Linda's barnyard hospital. Soon she was caring for pet dogs, pet cats, and even a pet goat.

Then, on her thirteenth birthday, Linda received a surprise present. Doc Currier stopped by and asked her to go with him on some sick calls.

Doc had remembered her wish! Linda scrambled up into the buggy, eager to get started.

In the months that followed Doc Currier often came to pick up his new helper. Sometimes they left the Sinclair house at sunrise and did not return until dark. As the buggy bumped along over the dirt roads, Linda asked questions.

"What is the best way to stop bleeding?"

"How can you tell if a bone is really broken?"

Doc Currier answered each question carefully. He knew Linda would try to remember every word he said.

At first Linda did only little tasks like boiling water and ripping bandage cloths. But before a year had passed, Doc Currier had shown her how to set splints on broken bones, clean wounds, and apply bandages.

"Treating sick people calls for calm and careful thinking," Doc Currier told Linda often. "Decide what needs to be done for your patient and do it. Sometimes you'll feel frightened. Just don't let your fear show. Your patient must trust you and have faith in you. Don't forget that."

One cold night a strange buggy stopped in front of the Sinclair farmhouse. Without tying his horse to the post, the driver leaped up the porch steps. He pounded on the door.

"We can't find Doc Currier," the worried young man told Grandpa Sinclair. "My wife said to come here and bring back the Richards girl who helps Doc. My boy's sick—real sick."

Linda heard the man. Even before grandpa could call her, she was putting on her coat. Soon Linda was hurrying through the doorway of a tiny white farmhouse. In the bedroom a woman sat beside a young boy.

"Oh, thank heavens, you've come. Tommy's so hot. He won't open his eyes. I don't know what to do."

Linda barely heard the woman's words. She saw that Tommy's skin was dry.

The boy was restless under the heavy quilt.

Linda tried to remember everything Doc Currier had told her about fever. She had never taken care of a patient without him. She was frightened, but there was no time to lose. She slipped off her coat and tossed it onto a nearby chair.

"We've got to break this fever," Linda declared, rolling up her sleeves. "We'll need chipped ice and towels."

Tommy's father hurried out into the snowy yard to hunt for chunks of ice. The boy's mother and Linda got the towels ready.

Moments later Linda filled a towel with ice chips. Then she stroked Tommy's head and chest with the cool, damp cloth.

Hour after hour Linda went on with

the ice baths. By morning her own body was tired and aching. But Tommy seemed cooler and more comfortable.

At last Doc Currier came. Linda ran to the door to meet him.

"I tried not to be afraid," she whispered in Doc's ear. "But I was— at first."

Slowly Doc Currier examined Tommy and asked Linda a few questions. Finally the old man stood up.

"Tommy is going to be just fine," he said. "He's a strong boy, and he's had a good nurse here. She did everything for him I could have done."

Linda felt happy at Doc's words. She knew she would never again be afraid to treat a patient.

Chapter *3*

The New Schoolmistress

The passing years brought many changes to the Sinclair farm. Grandma Sinclair died. Elizabeth married and moved away. Only Grandpa Sinclair and Linda were left.

"Linda, I've been thinking about your future," grandpa said one morning. "What's to become of you after I'm gone? I can't count on too many more years at my age."

Linda stopped clearing the breakfast dishes. She opened her mouth to speak. Grandpa did not give her the chance.

"I think this fall you should go to St. Johnsbury Academy. When you finish, you'll be able to teach."

"But I don't want to teach," Linda said. "I want to stay here with you."

Grandpa shook his head. "It would help me to know you're able to look after yourself. Anyway, I would feel proud if you were a teacher."

Linda accepted Grandpa Sinclair's wishes. At fifteen she enrolled in St. Johnsbury Academy. The school was thirty miles from Newport.

The year Linda spent at St. Johnsbury was an unhappy one. She hated the many lectures and daily tests. News of Doc Currier's death brought more sadness into the dreary year. Linda barely passed the state exams given at the end of the spring term. She was glad to return to the farm.

Linda wanted to teach near Newport so she could live with grandpa. Luckily she was hired as schoolmistress of the school she had once attended.

Linda braided her long dark hair and piled it high on her head. She wanted to look taller. She fixed up some of Grandma Sinclair's old dresses to wear.

A happy surprise greeted Linda on her first day at the schoolhouse. Many of her pupils were her old friends.

"Remember when you and Doc Currier fixed my leg?" one boy asked. "I'm going to pay you back by being good in school. Mama said I should."

"You and Doc Currier cured my sore throat," a girl with freckles said. "You took care of my baby doll too. Do you remember?"

Yes, Linda remembered. Linda often thought back to the house calls she

had made with Doc Currier. How happy and useful those days had been.

Linda had been teaching for only a year when Grandpa Sinclair died. In 1858 Linda sold the farm. Like other teachers of the time, she went to live with first one family, then another. Families were glad to give Linda a free room and meals in exchange for her teaching services.

In the summer of 1860 Linda went to live with an old widow outside Newport. Widow Poole was well known for her good cooking. No one enjoyed her fine meals more than her nephew George.

George Poole came to visit his aunt often. Linda liked him from the first time they met. George always had a funny story to tell. He took Linda ice skating and sledding. They sang songs in front of the fireplace. Linda liked being with George. When he asked her to marry him, Linda accepted. A May wedding date was set.

But one afternoon in April George came to the house early. He had bad news. Southern soldiers had fired on a United States Army fort filled with Northern soldiers. War was coming.

"Will you have to fight?" Linda asked.

"If President Lincoln calls for volunteers," George answered, "it would be my duty to go."

The call for volunteers came three days later. George Poole was among the first to sign up.

The Civil War lasted four years, and a million lives were lost. George Poole was badly wounded in the fighting. When he came home, he was weak and sickly. Once again Linda had a patient to nurse.

For almost five years Linda helped care for George. But George refused to marry her.

"I will not make you a bride one day and a widow the next," he said. His death in the winter of 1869 was a blow to Linda.

"My life is empty and without real meaning," she wrote to a friend. "Teaching is not the answer for me. It offers me no real happiness. I only hope I can find some useful purpose for my life."

Linda Richards decided that caring for the sick was the most useful work she could do. But if she were going to be a nurse, she wanted to be a good one. She knew she must find a place to get the training she needed.

Chapter *4*

On to Boston

Linda gripped her suitcase tightly as she stepped from the train in Boston. She knew no one in this big city. She had no place to work. She had no place to live. Linda was twenty-nine years old. She had been on her own for more than ten years. Still, she felt frightened. How long would her small savings last here?

Suddenly Linda remembered old Doc Currier's words: "Just don't let your fear show." Quickly Linda hurried out among the groups of strangers and into the street.

Linda had never seen so many tall buildings. She knew that some of them were hospitals and schools. Surely in one of them she could find the training she wanted. This hope made her forget her fear.

Linda found a room in a small boardinghouse. The owner was a friendly woman named Mrs. Higgens. She invited Linda to have a cup of tea with her, and soon Linda was talking about her plans. Mrs. Higgens looked doubtful.

"In England there are programs for training nurses," the landlady said. She sipped her warm tea. "I know of none in our country. Many doctors have boarded in my house, and I have heard their talk. I am quite certain that not one of them would have taken time to train women nurses."

"But what of the women who nursed the soldiers on the Civil War battlefields? Women nurses were useful then. Why couldn't they be useful now?"

Mrs. Higgens shook her head.

"The war is over now. Men believe that women belong in their homes, not in hospitals."

Linda refused to accept such an idea. She began looking for a nursing position in Boston's hospitals. Some doctors would not speak with her. Those who did were often rude.

"Me? Train a woman as a nurse? Never!" one doctor said.

"You have been trained as a teacher," was another doctor's reply. "Go home and teach!"

Linda kept looking. She pleaded for

any job that would give her hospital training. Finally she was offered work as a ward maid in the Boston City Hospital. The pay was only seven dollars a month, and she could not take care of sick people.

Still, she would be near the doctors and patients. She could learn by watching and listening. Linda took the job.

Linda began her duties at five o'clock every morning. She swept and scrubbed the floors. Then she washed windows, dusted, ironed sheets, and helped cook meals. Whenever she could she did favors for the patients.

One morning Linda brought a young boy a drink of water. Another ward maid was watching. She walked over to Linda and nudged her sharply in the side.

"Do the work you are told to do. Don't try to get out of your work by fussin' with the patients."

"What kind of hospital is this where the floors are treated better than the patients?" Linda wondered. She was more determined than ever to get some training.

The next morning Linda went to the head matron. She asked the older woman to teach her all that she had learned about caring for sick people. The head matron wanted to help. But she knew little more than Linda did.

Again and again Linda begged the doctors for help. Many of them laughed at her. A few became angry.

"You women are to take care of the cleaning. We will take care of the patients," one doctor declared.

"We could clean the hospital and help

you too if you would teach us," Linda answered firmly.

Linda worked sixteen hours a day, six days a week. She had no time to learn by watching the doctors. The head matron could not help her. Worn out and discouraged, she gave up her job.

"Get some rest and come back to us," the hospital director said. "We need good workers."

"A good worker. That's all I have been," Linda thought. "But I want to be more than that. I want to be a good nurse!"

As she rested and grew stronger, Linda read every book she could find about nursing. Stories about Florence Nightingale and her nursing programs in England gave Linda new hope. If only such programs could be brought to America!

At last Linda felt strong enough to begin her search for training again. A sign posted in a Boston bookstore caught her attention one day.

TRAINING PROGRAM FOR NURSES
OPENING SOON
THE NEW ENGLAND HOSPITAL FOR
WOMEN AND CHILDREN
PLEASANT STREET
BOSTON, MASSACHUSETTS

Linda hurried to Pleasant Street and found the hospital. She walked to the door and knocked.

"I've come about your training program for nurses," Linda said to the woman who opened the door.

"Just a moment," the woman answered. "I'll call Dr. Dimock. You may come into the parlor."

As she waited Linda wondered about this doctor. Why had he decided women should be trained as nurses? Maybe he had come from England.

Linda heard the parlor door open. In walked a tall young woman wearing a brown dress.

"I am Dr. Susan Dimock," she said. "I understand you have come about our training program for nurses."

A woman doctor? Linda was speechless.

"I—I'm sorry. I just didn't expect to meet a woman doctor."

Dr. Dimock smiled. "There are only a few of us in this country. If you're planning to become a nursing student, I hope you won't mind working with women doctors."

"If you don't mind working with women nurses," Linda laughed, "I won't mind working with women doctors."

Chapter *5*

Nursing School at Last

The nurses' training school was not going to open until fall. Linda did not want to wait so long to get started. She asked Dr. Dimock for summer work.

"We could use more help," Dr. Dimock agreed. "The hospital will be moving to a new building in October. But we have so little money. All we could give you would be meals and a bed—"

"I accept," Linda said quickly.

Linda became the hospital errand girl.

She wrote letters for the patients and read to them too. She helped cook meals and clean the hospital rooms.

On the morning of September 1, 1872, Linda was pounding nails into a wooden box. Moving day was only a few weeks away.

"Could you come into my office a minute, Linda?" Dr. Dimock called from her doorway.

Linda set the hammer and nails down. Wiping her damp face with her apron, she hurried into Dr. Dimock's office.

"I have something I want you to sign," Dr. Dimock said. She handed Linda a short piece of paper. "This is the day we begin our program for training nurses. Or had you forgotten?"

Linda shook her head as she took the enrollment form. She had looked forward to this moment for a long time. She signed the paper with the happy feeling that at last she was on her way.

"Linda, we are pleased that you are our first student nurse," Dr. Dimock said. "I know you will make us proud."

Soon four more women enrolled, and Dr. Dimock met with the five new students to explain the program. The young women were to wear simple housedresses and slippers. They must get up at 5:30 A.M. and stay on duty until 9:00 P.M. Each student nurse was to take care of six patients day and night. Each would receive one dollar a week for her services.

Early in the program the student nurses were taught to count pulse and breathing rates. Soon they learned to read and record temperatures. They

were shown how to measure and give medication.

Doctors gave speeches during the year. Each student nurse was expected to listen, watch, and remember everything she saw and heard.

The daily work was tiring, and the nights brought more problems. Again and again patients would call for their tired, sleepy nurses. Often the young women had only two or three hours of rest. Finally Linda went to Dr. Dimock.

"If one nurse could care for two wards during the night, the other could have a full night's rest. We could take turns sleeping and staying up," Linda suggested.

Dr. Dimock tried the plan at once and found that it worked well.

One night Linda was sent to the

home of a patient ill with pneumonia. A male doctor was treating the sick man when Linda arrived.

"I don't approve of women nurses," the doctor snapped. "You can be of little use to this patient."

Linda took off her cape and stood beside the patient's bed.

"If I can be of little use, it is better than no use at all," Linda said. "I will do my best to follow your orders."

The doctor liked Linda's answer. He agreed to let her try. For the next week Linda visited the patient twice a day. She cooked meals and gave medicine. She changed bedding and gave baths.

When the doctor made his next call he was pleased.

"This man is almost all well. I truly

didn't think you could do it," he told Linda.

"I am glad you think I have helped your patient," Linda said with dignity.

"*Our* patient," the doctor declared. "Yours *and* mine."

Before she knew it, Linda found herself at the end of the year's training. Again she was called to Dr. Dimock's office.

"Linda, this diploma shows you have successfully completed our nurses' training course. I am happy to give it to you." Dr. Dimock smiled. "You have done a fine job here. You have worked hard and have always given more than we asked of you. Your patients trust you and know that you care about them. I hope all our future students will try to do as well."

Linda stared at the words on the

diploma. Graduation day—September 1, 1873. At the age of thirty-two Linda was about to start a new life.

As news of Linda's graduation reached hospitals, offers of jobs began arriving. Not many doctors were willing to train nurses. But some were beginning to see that nurses could be useful. Linda read each offer carefully. After days of thought she made up her mind. She accepted the job of night nursing superintendent at the Bellevue Hospital Training School in New York City. Once again Linda knew she would be a stranger in a big city, but she was not afraid. The diploma—that piece of paper that said she was "a trained nurse"—made her feel she would succeed.

Chapter *6*

Battles To Win

Linda shuddered as she looked up at the huge building before her. The big iron gates seemed to shut the dark place off from the rest of the world.

Inside the hospital walls the patients also seemed shut off. They were the poor and hopeless people of New York City.

"I wish we could break down the walls of this place," Linda told the nursing director. "It's like an old tomb."

Sister Helen Bowden listened quietly.

A member of the English All Saints Order, she had studied nursing in London. She was trying to build a new program at Bellevue.

"Yes, it would be good to have a new hospital," she told Linda. "But there are other battles to win first." Sister Helen's voice rose in anger. "Our patients must be treated like human beings. You will learn soon enough what I mean."

Linda's first lesson came when she went on duty that night. The hospital gaslights were turned so low she couldn't make out the faces of the patients. All heat in the hospital was turned off at midnight. Linda looked for more blankets. There were none. For hours the patients shivered in the cold and darkness. Linda did her best to comfort them. Suddenly the heat was turned

on. The pipes cracked and rattled, waking everyone.

The next day Linda burst into Sister Helen's office.

"How can patients get well in a hospital where they freeze every night!" Linda cried. "Why must the lights be turned so low? How can student nurses be trained in a place like this?"

Sister Helen shook her head. "The members of the hospital board give the orders. They order the lights lowered. They order the heat turned off. They tell us to save money."

"Then we must show them the value of saving lives," said Linda.

Linda and Sister Helen became fighting partners. They went to every board meeting to ask for changes in the hospital.

Slowly the board members gave in.

Lights and heat were left on. A care center was opened so mothers and their new babies would not be near sick patients.

"I am both a pupil and teacher here," Linda wrote to Dr. Dimock. "I am learning many of the Nightingale training methods from Sister Helen. I teach classes every morning. Our student nurses are a cheerful group. One of them has made a uniform which the others· are now copying. It is a white and blue striped dress. A happy sight it is! It has a white collar, cuffs, and apron. A small white cap is worn so patients can see the students from a distance."

Student nurses at other training schools in America heard of the Bellevue uniforms. Before long each school of student nurses had its own uniform.

Linda thought it would be a good idea to keep a chart beside each patient's bed. Each time a nurse checked on a patient she marked the chart. When the doctor came, he could see at a glance whether the patient was getting better or worse. Soon other hospitals learned of the bed-chart idea and began using it.

At the end of Linda's year at Bellevue, Sister Helen urged her to stay on. But Linda felt she must help other hospitals set up nursing programs.

"There are battles to be won in many places," she told her partner. "I know you will keep fighting them here."

Linda was asked to lead the training program at the Massachusetts General Hospital. The program there was only one year old, and it was not going well. Linda sensed a challenge, so she accepted the job.

When she arrived at Massachusetts General, she found the doctors wanted nothing to do with a training school for nurses.

"It's a waste of time," they said.

Linda bristled when she heard such comments. Yet she kept her temper, for she wanted to win the doctors' friendship. Besides, Linda had a plan.

She invited relatives and friends of the doctors to afternoon teas. Members of the hospital board were guests too.

"You are all interested in Massachusetts General Hospital," Linda told those attending. "So am I. So are the student nurses who are with us today. I'm sure you'll want to hear about the work they hope to do in the hospital."

The student nurses were excited about their work. They talked for hours with their guests.

"If the doctors help teach us, the patients will receive better care. We will ease the doctors' work load too," said the student nurses.

Linda's plan worked. Her guests went back to the doctors to urge them to help the eager young students. Finally, the doctors agreed.

With the help of the doctors, Linda set up a one-year program for training nurses. New workers were hired to clean and cook—jobs the student nurses once had to do.

"Now let us prove how useful we can be," Linda told her classes.

When her first class of student nurses graduated in 1875, Linda watched with a happy smile. Her smile was even brighter as she looked around at the doctors. They were all proud of *their* school for nurses.

More training schools were opening in America each year. Many of them wanted Linda to help plan their programs. But Linda was ready for a change.

For a long time Linda had heard about the Nightingale Training School in London. Now and then visitors from America were allowed to go there to learn about the programs. Linda wrote a letter asking if she might be accepted.

Months went by. No answer came. Linda had almost given up hope. Then a letter arrived from London.

"My dear Miss Richards,
The Nightingale Training School at St. Thomas's Hospital would be happy to have you as a visitor. We shall look forward to meeting you."

Chapter 7

A Special Invitation

Linda sailed from New York City in April 1877. A tall stranger was waiting to meet her at the dock in England.

"I am Mr. Rathbone from the school at St. Thomas's," the man said. He took Linda to his carriage. "We are happy to welcome you to England. My cousin, Miss Florence Nightingale, sends her special greetings."

Linda's face showed surprise. She hadn't expected such attention from the famous Miss Nightingale.

A few days later Linda received

another surprise—a note inviting her to lunch. The invitation was signed by Florence Nightingale.

Linda slept little the night before the luncheon. She was too excited. Again and again she changed her mind about what dress to wear. She scolded herself as she braided her hair into a soft bun at the back of her head.

"You are thirty-six years old, not a schoolgirl of ten," Linda told herself. "You are just going to visit another nurse."

Still, as she walked up the front steps of Florence Nightingale's house on South Street, Linda's heart beat faster. A maid led her into the sitting room.

Florence Nightingale was resting on a small velvet couch. She was almost sixty, but her face was smooth and without the usual lines of age.

"Miss Richards, I am so happy you could come," she said with a smile.

Linda suddenly was at ease. At once she felt Florence Nightingale was her friend.

All afternoon the two women talked. Miss Nightingale helped Linda make plans for learning about the Nightingale program.

The study began at St. Thomas's Training School. Linda was met by the matron, Mrs. Wardroper.

"We want you to stay right here with us at the nurses' home," said Mrs. Wardroper. "You will spend one week in each of our hospital's eight wards. You may work or watch as you choose. You may attend all surgical operations and staff meetings."

Linda reported for duty early the next morning in the children's ward.

"You must be the American nurse," one doctor declared. "Jolly good! Glad to have you with us."

Linda nodded. She was happy the doctors seemed so kind. There was so much she wanted to learn.

At St. Thomas's Linda worked in each of the eight wards. Every day she spent a busy twelve hours on duty. Then, at night in her room, Linda kept her desk lamp burning late as she wrote down all she had seen and heard.

"Both the patient and doctor trust the nurses here," she wrote. "I believe this trust helps the nurses carry out their duties."

Linda visited other hospitals. Sometimes she went to nursing classes. Other times she worked in the hospital wards. Always she carried a notebook in her apron pocket.

"You must get tired of writing," one nurse said.

Linda nodded. "It's just that I don't want to forget anything. We in America have much to learn from you."

As Linda's stay in England ended, she received another invitation from Florence Nightingale to spend a few days at her summer home.

Linda was happy to see Miss Nightingale again. Each afternoon they met for tea and talked in the garden. The two women became good friends.

From England, Linda went to Paris. There she spent a month visiting hospitals and schools. But now she was eager to return to America to share what she had learned. In October 1877 Linda sailed for home.

Chapter 8

Journey to Japan

Good news was waiting for Linda on her arrival in America. Six more hospitals had started training programs for nurses. Another was ready to begin at Boston City Hospital. The hospital director asked Linda to lead the program.

"Most of our doctors are against the idea of a training school for nurses," said Dr. Cowles. "You'll have a lot of hard work here. Getting the doctors to help will be the hardest part of all. But I will do all I can for you."

It was not an easy decision for Linda. She remembered how unhappy she had been at Boston City Hospital. But she could not say no to a challenge.

"I accept your offer," Linda told Dr. Cowles. "We'll show those other doctors how useful good nurses can be!"

Linda set up a two-year program for training nurses. She used many ideas she had learned in England and from Florence Nightingale.

Since the Boston City Hospital doctors would not help, Linda looked for teachers in other places. She brought in graduate nurses from other hospitals to lead classes. Linda taught some of the classes too.

Often after class a group of students gathered around Linda to talk. She listened to their problems. She gave them good advice.

"Always remember, the care of your patient must come first," she told her students. "You must hide your own problems when you are working. Be ready to help the doctors quickly whenever they need you." The young women soon learned to love and respect Linda. They listened eagerly to all she told them.

Slowly the students began to win the trust of the doctors. More and more duties were given the new nurses. Finally the doctors agreed to help with the program.

Once the program was accepted and running well, Linda began to look around for a new task. She heard that someone was needed to set up a nursing program in Japan. Linda volunteered for the job.

"I know nothing of the Japanese

language or customs," she said. "But I'm willing to help if I can."

Linda was accepted. She sailed for Japan in December 1885.

Before she started to plan the nursing program, Linda studied the Japanese language. Before long she could speak well enough to begin teaching.

But not all Japanese customs came so easily. After watching her fumble with her chopsticks while eating, Linda's friends gave her a special gift.

"Linda, here is a wooden spoon," they said. "The food you can keep on your chopsticks wouldn't keep an ant alive."

Linda put her chopsticks aside with a hearty laugh.

"You've probably saved me from death by starvation," she admitted.

The school for nurses was set up in a small mission hospital in Kyoto. It was Linda's job to plan a two-year program. She was pleased to find she would have the help of two American mission doctors and six Japanese doctors.

Five students enrolled in the first class. They shared two tiny rooms behind the kitchen in the mission hospital. Linda had her own little room upstairs near three small rooms for the hospital patients.

"Our school and hospital is tiny," Linda told the new students. "But sometimes a tiny bottle of medicine can do much good."

Linda spoke slowly in Japanese. Often it was easier for her to explain things in English. She was happy to find that two of the students spoke English and could help the other three.

While the students learned more about nursing, Linda learned more about

Japanese customs. She discovered that the student nurses were sometimes afraid of the men patients.

"In Japan woman never tell Japanese man what to do," one student told Linda one day. "Today my man patient won't take medicine."

Linda had long ago learned to handle all kinds of problems with patients.

"Come with me," she said, leading the way to a mat where a Japanese man lay. "Now, when the nurse gives you medicine, it is what the doctor has told her to do," she said to the man. "The nurse is not telling you to take medicine. The doctor is."

The man nodded and took the medicine willingly. His dignity was saved.

"Ah, that is better," the student smiled.

The mission hospital and school for

nurses in Kyoto grew fast. Linda went into the city and taught home nursing to other Japanese students.

Linda stayed in Japan for five years. Then an ear ailment began to bother her. The hospital doctors said she should return to America.

With some sadness Linda packed her bags. She smiled as she slipped the old wooden spoon into her suitcase. She would miss her Japanese friends.

Chapter 9

Home Nursing

A brisk November wind snapped at Linda's dark cape as she hurried along the Philadelphia street. Linda looked again at the numbers on the nearby tenement houses.

"Down here, lady!" a child's voice called out.

Quickly Linda walked down the steps to a basement doorway. She smiled at the little girl who had come to the visiting nurse's office that morning.

"Where is your papa?" Linda asked.

"Come. I take you to him." The girl

took Linda's hand and led her inside. "Papa will not be happy I bring you. He thinks you ladies snoop in our houses. He thinks you laugh at us for being poor."

Linda shook her head. "We want only to help you if we can. I will talk with your papa. Don't be frightened."

On a cot in the next room Linda found the man tossing in a restless sleep. Linda stepped closer. She could see a deep and dirty cut between two of the fingers on his right hand. Red streaks shot up his badly swollen arm.

Suddenly the man's eyes opened.

"Who are you? What do you want here?" he asked.

"I am Miss Richards of the Philadelphia Visiting Nurses." Linda set her nursing bag on a table. "I have come to help you. Please let me see—"

"Get out! Get out of here!" the man shouted. "If I wanted help, I would send for a doctor."

It was hopeless to argue. Linda took her bag and left. But in an hour she was back—with a doctor. He examined the man's wound and turned to Linda.

"The wound is just as you told me, Miss Richards. The treatment you plan to use is exactly right. Yes, by all means put hot, wet cloths on the wound to draw the poison. When the poison has gathered, open the wound."

"This—this woman can do that?" the patient asked.

"Probably better than I could!" the doctor laughed. "Now you do as she says."

Linda had joined the Philadelphia Visiting Nurses Society soon after returning from Japan. The nurses traveled all over the city to care for sick people in their homes. Most of their work was done in poor areas of the city. Linda liked that, for she felt most useful when she was helping the poor.

The Philadelphia society had its share of problems. The visiting nurses needed money for their work. The money was given by wealthy families in the city. Some people began saying the visiting nurses could not be "of good character." They said no nice woman would go about the city alone and into the homes of poor strangers. Also, many of the poor families did not trust the nurses who offered free help.

Linda became head nurse in April 1891. She attacked the problems right away.

Linda called at the homes of the wealthy families. She told the people of the work of the visiting nurses.

Often Linda met with the visiting nurses. "When you enter a home, do nothing but care for your patient. Do not speak about or even notice other things in the home," she told them.

Slowly the stories about the visiting nurses disappeared. The poor families began to welcome the visiting nurses.

But for Linda the price of success had been high. The home visits, the long reports that had to be written, the direction of the program—all had tired her.

Once again Linda had worked so hard that she become ill. Now fifty, she had nursed for many long and wearing years. She knew she must rest for a while. But she also knew that before long there would be a new challenge. And when it came she would not be able to say no.

Chapter *10*

A Final Task

Linda listened quietly to the two men who had come to see her. They wanted her to become director of nurses at a hospital for the mentally ill.

"I would like to help you," Linda said. "But I have worked only with general nursing programs. I don't know if I have the skills for the work you want done."

"Let *us* judge your skills, Miss Richards. We know you can help us."

Linda could not refuse. As the nineteenth century ended, Linda became director of nurses at a mental hospital in Taunton, Massachusetts.

Linda worked closely with the doctors. They tried new ways of treating the mentally ill patients. Linda shared what she learned with the student nurses.

"Take time to listen to your patients," Linda told the students. "Help them to become interested in doing something. Be gentle and kind. These people are lonely and afraid, but do not pity them. Talk with them. They must feel you care about them."

Linda spent little time in her office. She liked working with the patients.

One day as a doctor walked out of the hospital he saw Linda high on a ladder against a tree. Three patients were firmly holding the ladder.

"Miss Richards, what are you doing?" the doctor called.

"I am hanging our birdhouses," Linda called down. "We made them in the hospital workshop."

The nurses at Taunton followed Linda's example. They spent time talking with the patients and helping them do small chores.

Linda helped start nursing programs for the mentally ill at other hospitals. But the years were slipping by. Linda knew she could not keep up the busy pace of her younger days. In 1911, at seventy, Linda gave up active nursing.

Linda went to live quietly with friends in Foxboro, Massachusetts. She was always glad to welcome guests but seldom left her house.

In 1928 Linda became ill and was taken to a nursing home. When the nurses at the New England Hospital for Women and Children heard of Linda's

illness, they begged her to come stay with them.

So it was that Linda returned to the hospital from which she had graduated as America's first trained nurse. She died there April 16, 1930.

Newspapers across the country carried the news of Linda's death. Some noted the final words of her autobiography, which was published in 1912:

> "As for my own work, I often feel that, for the many years I have served, I have accomplished little. Whether I have been a wise builder, someone else must decide."

Was Linda a "wise builder?"
For the answer, one has only to look at the profession of nursing today.

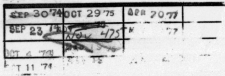